The Cat Made Me Buy It!

A Collection of
Cats Who Sold Yesterday's Products

5 CENTS

written and designed by
ALICE L. MUNCASTER & ELLEN YANOW

PHOTOGRAPHY BY CHUCK WOOD

CROWN PUBLISHERS, INC.

New York

To Fancy and Ruby, our first cats,
who introduced us to friendship
and inspired this book

Published by Crown Publishers, Inc., One Park Avenue, New York, New York 10016,
and simultaneously in Canada by
General Publishing Company Limited
Manufactured in Hong Kong

Library of Congress Cataloging in Publication Data

Muncaster, Alice L.
The cat made me buy it!

1. Cats in advertising—History.   I. Yanow, Ellen.
II. Wood, Chuck.   III. Title.
HF5827.M86   1984   659.1'96368'009   84-4241

ISBN 0-517-55338-4

10   9   8   7   6   5   4   3   2

The Cats Who Sold Yesterday's Products

e'd like to ask you a question: Do you think a cat could make you buy a pair of shoes? What about a box of chocolates—or a magazine? Unless you believe cats have some sort of magical power over people, your answer may be "not very likely." But we'd like to introduce you to some very special cats who may convince you otherwise.

They are the cats who sold yesterday's products—four-footed salesmen who appeared in advertising as much as a hundred years ago. Their purpose was to influence consumer behavior—in short, to persuade people to buy the products they represented.

As unusual as it may sound, the cat was very effective in this role. Cats are excellent attention-getters—and as people noticed the cats in these advertisements, they noticed the products, too. According to advertising people, getting noticed is the first step toward making a sale to the customer, so the cat played a very important part in the success of these ads.

But why a cat? Cats were probably first added to advertising as one of many different illustrations used to attract the eye of potential buyers. Over the years, advertisers experimented with all sorts of ways to get people's attention. The cat just happened to work better than a lot of other ideas.

Today, that feline appeal is an accepted truth, verified by consumer researchers. An ad is more likely to be noticed if it contains a likeness of a cat than if it features many other images; in test situations, people look first at pictures of adults and children, then at pictures of animals such as cats.

Cats also have a long history of friendship

The cat in the Kitty Kat shoes symbol comes to life in this beautifully illustrated advertising postcard. The James Clark Leather Company made a series of interesting cards for its dealers to send to customers. The cards were also offered as a collector's set, for just a postage charge of two cents. The St. Louis, Missouri, company was founded in 1896 and also made leatherworking tools and shoe store supplies and fixtures for several decades.

4

with mankind—a fact frequently dramatized by the presence of cats in art and literature. So it is not unusual to find kittens and cats in advertising, especially when you consider that advertising, like art and literature, reflects the life-style of the times, including people, home life, work, play, and even pets.

The cats you are about to meet all date from the late 1800s through the 1950s. This was a time when the printed word was the main form of communication in America—well before electronic media rose to the great importance they have today. It was also the time when advertising was characterized by artists' illustrations rather than photography.

The advertising you will see from before the turn of the century is from the beginning of the "modern" age of advertising—an era that provided us with some of the loveliest examples of advertising cats. We chose this starting point because technological breakthroughs in the printing industry occurred during this time, including the first mechanical typesetting, faster printing presses, and high-quality color lithography. Almost overnight this changed the way people learned about products. At the same time, improved transportation, provided mainly by the rapidly developing railroads, brought products from far away to virtually every American consumer. So companies large and small began to advertise profusely—providing for the first time in history an opportunity for cats to be widely seen in advertising—and they were immediately used to help sell products as diverse as thread, foods, soap, cigars, and games.

Into the twentieth century, cats remained enormously popular, often being featured in large, beautiful advertising illustrations, more likely than not in full color. As new industries and businesses flourished, so did the use of the

Mavis advertisements were familiar to readers of 1920s' women's magazines. This one for Mavis Talc appeared in *Ladies' Home Journal* in July 1923. The drawing is one of a series by popular illustrators commissioned by the Vivaudou Company for use in its advertising. The company also created "Mavis, the Irresistible Waltz" in 1920 and offered it to the public as sheet music, a phonograph record, or a player piano roll. Mavis Talc is still produced today, as one of the many toiletries made by The Nestle-LeMur Company.

Packers in cigar factories put an outer label on the end of each filled cigar box. This unusual oval end label was designed in 1909 by W. C. Smith of Windsor, Pennsylvania. Its border appears to have a finish of thinly applied gold (gold leaf), but skilled printers who specialized in early lithographed labels could achieve this effect by mixing less-expensive bronze powder into printing ink.

CATS ARE NICE...

But Cat-arrh isn't nice and any one who has it should use

COLMAN'S EMOLLIENT.

JANUARY 1895

SUN	MON	TUE	WED	THU	FRI	SAT
		1	2	3	4	5
6	7	8	9	10	11	12
13	14	15	16	17	18	19
20	21	22	23	24	25	26
27	28	29	30	31		

For Free Sample Send to

Kittens had a double purpose on this 1895 calendar. They were cute enough to please Victorian ladies, who saved colorful printed keepsakes, and they illustrated a play on the word *catarrh*—a catchphrase for many types of respiratory infections of this era, supposedly due to an "impure condition of the blood." Colman's Emollient was a patent medicine promoted as relieving irritation of the throat and lungs. It was one of many products made by the Colman family, prominent in Kalamazoo, Michigan, from the late 1840s to the late 1930s.

cat in advertising—as they promoted inventive products, such as mass-produced clothing and even automotive supplies.

Of course, the cat was more important to the success of some products than to others along the way. Some companies may have produced only a single advertisement featuring a cat. Others, however, firmly linked their corporate identity to the cat—giving cat-related names to their products, or even to the entire company.

On the pages ahead, you'll find advertising for Kaliko Kat shoes, Tabby cigars, Tom Cat oranges, Black Cat hosiery, and White Cat underwear, to name a few examples. And some corporate relationships with cats were even immortalized by product trademarks—with an image of a cat sometimes stamped onto or sewn into the goods themselves.

As you become better acquainted with our beautiful persuaders, you may wonder if any of them had real-life counterparts. We had hoped so but, as we searched to discover the story behind each cat, we found the answer elusive.

Many companies today do not have information about their early advertising. Some, sadly, have lost irreplaceable records in transitions and disasters; other companies are no longer in existence. And the artists, for the most part, are also untraceable. They usually

sold their work anonymously—just as most advertising artists and writers do today—to manufacturers, retailers, advertising agencies, and printing companies. Even when designs were copyrighted, they were almost never registered by the artist.

So the truth may never be known. Unfortunately, it is not possible to ask the illustrators or their descendants if the cats were fashioned after live models that may have pranced around the artists' drawing boards.

But, as anyone who has ever lived with a cat will agree, it is very difficult to capture the beauty and grace of the feline—in art or in words—without the intimate knowledge and understanding that come from close personal contact with a cat. So we suspect that many of the artists simply glanced across their studios to view the inspiration for their illustrations.

As you will soon see, the cat appeared in many different promotional forms, and especially during the years represented in this book—when television and radio were not yet available to everyone—advertisers found many creative ways to reach the public with their product messages. We have included selections from each of the following categories:

Magazine advertisements   The magazine was an important medium seventy-five to a

Illustrations of flowers or vegetables could always be found on the covers of old seed catalogs, but this 1893 cover was unusual because a child and a cat were also featured. John Salzer carefully carried supplies of his favorite seeds with him when he immigrated to America from Germany. His seed business, begun as a hobby in 1868, grew into a thriving mail-order firm through diligent advertising. Salzer died in 1891, and his heirs guided the company into the twentieth century. The company went out of business in the 1950s.

hundred years ago, to advertisers and the public alike. To be seen by the rapidly expanding population of the late 1800s and early 1900s, companies selected popular magazines of the day with circulations that were national in scope. Cats were used to interest many distinct audiences. Our examples are from magazines for women, men, and children.

Signs and posters   Companies that used cats in advertising often extended the theme to other promotional formats. Included here are large signs and posters, designed for use in store windows, on walls, or outdoors, as well as smaller counter-top displays. They might have been seen at department stores in large cities or at general stores and country stores in small-town and rural America. Some were made for specialty outlets, such as tobacco or fabric shops.

Advertising trade cards   Shoppers at stores in the 1880s and 1890s usually took home at least one advertising trade card for their collections. These colorfully printed cards with illustrations of flowers, children, animals (including cats), and products in use were extremely popular advertising devices for manufacturers and retailers. The cards evolved (and took their name) from the tradesman's cards of the eighteenth century, which described craftsmen's occupations and services. Victorian women and children avidly collected advertising cards, which put beautifully colored pictures in the hands of the general public for the first time. By 1900, however, the novelty of advertising cards had worn off, and they virtually disappeared from use. Another type of card, the advertising postcard, was mailed in later years by companies and salesmen to retailers and customers alike. We have shown examples from the early 1900s.

Packaging   Boxes, bottles, jars, and other types of product packages have provided companies yet another opportunity to advertise, or catch the shopper's attention, year after year. At the point of sale, an appealing design on the package or label—one made familiar by advertising—could help a customer decide which brand to purchase.

Premiums and giveaways   Another effective promotional tactic teamed up with cats has been the use of premiums. Companies gave consumers a wide variety of complimentary merchandise over the years—imprinted with product or sales messages—to keep an advertising reminder constantly in the consumer's view. Calendars, metal trays, lapel pins, mirrors, and ink blotters were but a few of the many popular premiums on which cats made appearances.

Magazine covers   Cats were featured on numerous magazine covers since before the turn of the century. They could catch the eye of the passerby with their interesting and unusual poses, and this helped a customer decide which magazine to buy—the one with the cat on the cover, of course.

Sheet music   The cat's popularity also extended into the music of the 1800s and early 1900s. Music publishers promoted many songs and melodies with illustrations of cats on the covers of sheet music.

All of the items photographed for this book reside permanently in our two private collections. Many are extremely rare; some are one-of-a-kind. They have never before been assembled for public display.

These charming creatures were awaiting discovery for as long as a century in basements, attics, garages, warehouses, and file drawers across America. We discovered them one by one—along with hundreds of others—in searches that began over a decade ago. Perhaps our first finds were purely by chance, but our continuing search is more a passion—one we can explain only as "the cats make us buy them!"

With each new discovery, we become more convinced of the cat's interesting role in advertising—a role that has not been formally acknowledged until now. We hope you will enjoy meeting these cats who sold yesterday's products and captured our hearts. We find them just too beautiful not to be shared.

From the 1880s until about 1950, fruit was shipped from grower to grocer in wooden crates. Colorful labels identified the brands and types of fruit inside, such as this one for Persian brand apples, from the 1930s. The lithographers who designed and produced these outstanding labels used thousands of different illustrations, including people, scenery, and animals. The C. C. Smith Fruit Company of Yakima and Wenatchee, Washington, first used the "Persian" name in 1928. This label's background color designated fancy-grade fruit; blue was used for extra fancy, and green or white for good grades. This delightful brand of apples is, unfortunately, no longer produced.

ats were popular as illustrations on colorful sheet music published from around the turn of the century through the 1920s. From ragtime tunes to jazz, cats walked, stalked, pranced, posed, and serenaded each other on the covers of hundreds of song sheets.

It was a time when people turned mostly to music for entertainment. In 1900 the automobile was still a relatively new invention, but millions of people owned pianos. Playing the parlor piano became a popular national pastime. By 1920 America had been through a devastating World War, but radio was still in its infancy as an entertainer. Traveling minstrel and vaudeville shows were in vogue, combining comedy acts with the newest songs of the day. Sheet music sales flourished.

Love songs were the favorites, along with patriotic songs during the war years—but many songs were written about cats. Some were tributes to loved pets. Some were melodies that tried to capture the grace of feline movement. There were a number of vaudeville-style comedy spoofs, and even

trendy musical selections and dance fads were teamed up with the cat—such as "The Black Cat Rag" and "Pussyfoot Fox Trot."

Cat illustrations were so graphically different from the usual cover themes that they stood out in the crowd—they were easy to notice in the music store and on the pages of mail-order music catalogs. Being seen, of course, was the first step toward making a sale, so sometimes publishers even put cats on the covers of song sheets that had nothing to do with cats.

By the 1930s, however, things had changed. When the movies learned to talk, they created a new mood for the nation. Musical extravaganzas filled theater screens. The sheet music industry followed the trend, and during the 1930s and '40s song sheets from the movies flourished. Many covers featured scenes from motion pictures or photos of movie stars. But sales declined anyway, as people paid more attention to the radio or phonograph than to making their own music.

Today, the "cat songs" are gone, but the lavishly illustrated sheet music lingers on as a cherished memento of another time.

Paper cat faces from the 1930s open up to reveal mirrors that tuck away in a pocket or purse. Such novelty items were usually produced by a printing firm or advertising specialty company and sold as a customer giveaway item to many different businesses—custom-imprinted with an advertising message. The mirror on the left advertised an optometrist's services; the one on the right promoted a beauty salon.

Serenading cats have inspired many popular songs and interesting sheet music covers. When this sheet music was published in 1919, comedy songs were the rage. The "ME-OW Song" tells the story of a cat named Angora and his noisy nighttime antics.

ME-OW
Song
50
Words by
Harry D. Kerr
Music by
Mel B. Kaufman
Sam Fox Pub. Co.
Cleveland
EUROPEAN REPRESENTATIVES. BOSWORTH & CO. LONDON

he cigar in America was never more popular than in Victorian times. By the 1880s, almost twenty thousand brands were being produced in the United States. In almost every town, a smoker had hundreds of choices available—many made in small local factories.

With the passing of legislation in 1865 requiring cigars to be packaged for easier tax calculation, boxes began to line the shelves of tobacco shops. This sparked manufacturers to start using the end panel and the inside of the lid for brand identification and advertising messages.

Cigar companies commissioned artists to design special box labels and also purchased blank labels from printers on which their brand names could be imprinted. In both cases, beautiful labels resulted—with scenes and titles as diverse as the pastimes and pleasures of the people who created them. Beautiful women were popular subjects, as were sports, famous people, American scenes, home life, buildings, gambling, plants, and animals.

Cats were pictured in a variety of designs, probably because cats were part of the Victorian household, and because—with their natural beauty and grace—they made interesting artistic subjects.

Cigar boxes that have survived the years were often those that were saved for storing household items. Boxes featuring cats undoubtedly appealed to Victorian women and children—and these boxes were likely to be treasured and kept around the home so that the pictures on the labels could be enjoyed again and again.

Some cigars were packaged as pairs, held together with a large cigar band, such as this "Two Toms" wrapper.

Three varieties of wooden cigar boxes with a feline theme: "CATS," a Victorian scene, by Brener Brothers, London, Ontario, Canada, from the turn of the century; "Old Tom," ca. 1900, which used the name of a type of sweetened gin popular in Victorian times; and "Pussy," ca. 1910–16, a classic white cat introduced in 1908 by K. H. Jacobs of Windsor, Pennsylvania. These cigar boxes were made to hold small cigars.

Artistic variety and brilliant chromolithography
characterize many old cigar box labels. These examples
are of the type affixed to the inside lid of a cigar box
when the box was manufactured. The sophisticated
"TABBY" is an 1894 design from the H. Traiser
Company, a Boston distributor. The intense rivals on
the "ME-OW" label were designed by Austin-Nichols
& Company, New York City, in 1886. The "White-
Cat" label is one of several styles with this title
produced between 1888 and 1908.

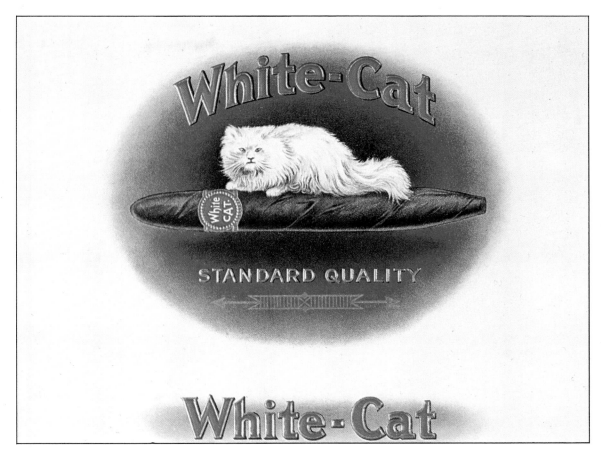

Kaliko Kat Shoes from the International Shoe Co., St. Louis, had a stylized calico cat trademark. This celluloid advertising pin from the mid-1920s could be worn on a collar or lapel. Another popular promotional item given away at shoe stores during this time was a tin clicker (noisemaker) on which the "Kaliko Kat" had been lithographed.

Coca-Cola had already been quenching thirst for thirty-eight years when this advertisement appeared in popular women's magazines in 1924. It creatively adapted a line from the writings of William Shakespeare: "One touch of nature makes the whole world kin."

Coca-Cola syrup was concocted in 1886 by Dr. John Styth Pemberton, an Atlanta pharmacist—supposedly in a pot in his backyard. That year, sales averaged thirteen glasses a day at a local soda fountain. In 1889 the company began to advertise, and throughout the years since then it has consistently devoted large sums of money to advertising and promotion. Today, people around the world consume over eight billion gallons of Coke every year. The familiar bottle on the table was first used in 1916.

Thirst
is a touch
of nature
that makes
the whole
world kin

REFRESH YOURSELF · DRINK COCA-COLA DELICIOUS AND REFRESHING 5¢

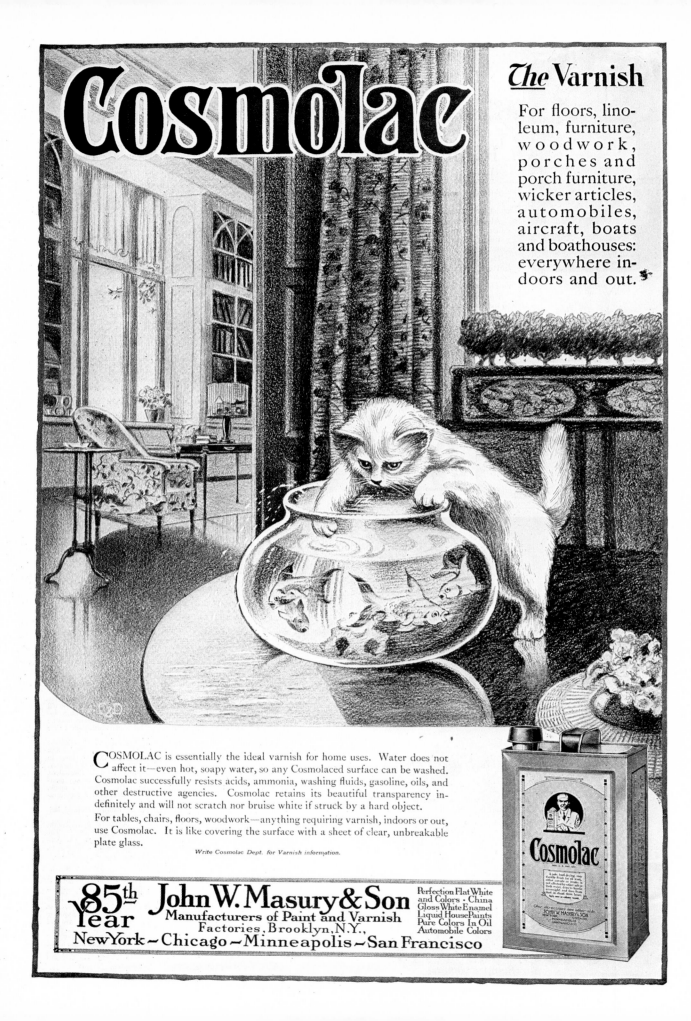

Cosmolac

The Varnish

For floors, linoleum, furniture, woodwork, porches and porch furniture, wicker articles, automobiles, aircraft, boats and boathouses: everywhere indoors and out.

COSMOLAC is essentially the ideal varnish for home uses. Water does not affect it—even hot, soapy water, so any Cosmolaced surface can be washed. Cosmolac successfully resists acids, ammonia, washing fluids, gasoline, oils, and other destructive agencies. Cosmolac retains its beautiful transparency indefinitely and will not scratch nor bruise white if struck by a hard object.

For tables, chairs, floors, woodwork—anything requiring varnish, indoors or out, use Cosmolac. It is like covering the surface with a sheet of clear, unbreakable plate glass.

Write Cosmolac Dept. for Varnish information.

85th Year **John W. Masury & Son**
Manufacturers of Paint and Varnish
Factories, Brooklyn, N.Y.,
New York ~ Chicago ~ Minneapolis ~ San Francisco

Perfection Flat White and Colors · China Gloss White Enamel
Liquid House Paints
Pure Colors In Oil
Automobile Colors

Because color printing was still somewhat of a novelty in the 1890s, colorful advertising cards like this one for E. W. Hoyt & Co. (1894) were popular with the public and were eagerly saved. Hoyt's Cologne is still produced and is sold mostly on the East Coast by the J. Strickland Company of Memphis, Tennessee. Hoyt's Rubifoam, once a widely used flavored tooth polish, is no longer made.

The reader's eye was cleverly drawn to the polished tabletop by a curious kitten in this advertisement for Cosmolac varnish. The John W. Masury & Son Company placed the ad in the October 1919 issue of *Ladies' Home Journal.* The company is now owned by the Valspar Corporation.

lack Cat Stove Polish helped keep turn-of-the-century stoves gleaming and rust-free. Kitchen and potbelly stoves of the late 1800s and early 1900s were made mostly of cast iron, and household chores included applying a carbon- or graphite-based polish regularly to their surfaces, for protection from water, grease, and rust.

The polish was produced as a paste—packaged in a small round metal container—and as a liquid. The cat face on the label made the Black Cat brand instantly recognizable to customers in hardware and general stores, where stove polishes were usually sold.

Black Cat was one of many stove polishes made by the J. L. Prescott Company. The name was also used for another product—Black Cat Shoe Polish, introduced in 1912.

The Prescott Company, which was founded in 1870, is still in existence. Black Cat Stove Polish was made until 1970.

Both Black Cat Stove Polish and Black Cat Shoe Polish were advertised by this celluloid pin-back button, which was given free to customers.

The even coloring and subtle glossy coat of a real-life black cat may have been the inspiration for the Black Cat brand name. The cat's prominence in advertising Black Cat Stove Polish helped distinguish this brand from its competition. The sign shown measures 11″ x 15½″. *Left:* Two versions of the Black Cat Stove Polish bottle show how it changed over the years. The bottle with the cork stopper is from before 1896, when the company moved to Passaic, New Jersey. With the newer twist-off cap came a decrease in capacity—from seven ounces to six.

20

BLACK CAT

ENAMEL STOVE POLISH

OUTSHINES' EM ALL

MANUFACTURED BY
J.L. PRESCOTT CO. NEW YORK

No. 51-A

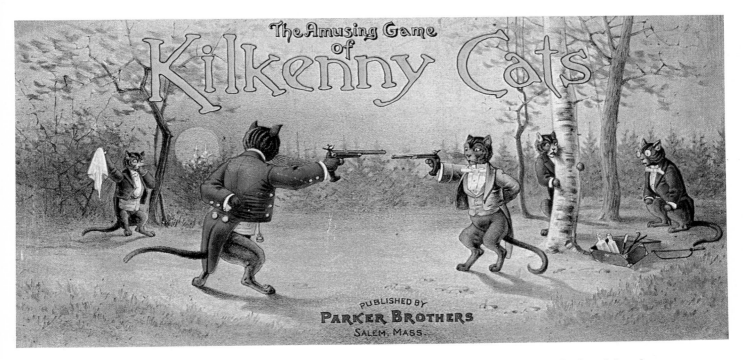

The Amusing Game of Kilkenny Cats was made by Parker Brothers from 1890 to 1898. The box lid and game board featured gentlemanly dueling cats, and the object of the game was to capture all eight game pieces belonging to the opponent. The game was named for the Kilkenny cats that, according to an old English ballad, fought until they both disappeared. Parker Brothers has been making games for more than a hundred years in Salem, Massachusetts.

t one time or another, some of the world's most prominent manufacturers of games have created charming pastimes that revolved around cats.

Nursery rhymes and folklore lent ideas for games, as did favorite tests of skill. Many games were enjoyed by adults as well as children, and they were so popular that the companies offered them for decades.

Cats were quite popular game subjects in the Victorian era, and illustrations on the lids of game boxes from the turn of the century were particularly interesting. Cats were often dressed up in the colorful, flowing costumes of the times. Sometimes the feline characters drawn on the game box cover also appeared on the board or on playing pieces inside.

Puzzles, too, helped many youngsters and families pass the time on rainy afternoons and cold winter nights. Favorite themes were lively cartoon-style cats in playful or mischievous situations, or all dressed up in Sunday-best clothing—much like those found on the pages of children's books in the 1880–1910 period.

Most of the beautiful Victorian games and puzzles were discarded when children grew up, but those that were packed away by sentimental parents are delightful discoveries today.

Little Kittens Tidley Winks was produced around 1930 by J. W. Spear and Son Ltd., a British game manufacturer. The small, flat counters were flipped toward the stand-up cats, and a player scored if the disk landed in a cat's mouth and fell from a numbered chute. Spear's games have been made for 106 years, and the grandson of the founder directs the company today.

"The Cat Congress" is a framed advertising sign for Clark's O.N.T. thread. It was made in the 1880s; the initials O.N.T. meant "Our New Thread." Cats also appeared on Clark's thread advertising cards in the 1875–1900 period. Cats love to play with string, so many thread manufacturers of the past called upon cats to "demonstrate" their product in advertising illustrations. Over the years, many of these companies—including Clark's major competitor, the J. & P. Coats Company—consolidated to become what is now Coats & Clark, Inc. Both the Clark and Coats families produced thread in Scotland in the early 1800s before establishing U.S. operations in the mid-1800s. "The Cat Congress" measures 23¼″ x 16¼″.

Lawson Wood, a popular British illustrator of the 1930s and '40s, drew this whimsical 1939 cover for *Collier's* magazine. Wood's covers were known for their artistic humor during this era, fifty years after *Collier's* began publication as a general-interest magazine. The last issue of *Collier's* appeared in 1957.

June 3, 1939

Collier's

THE NATIONAL WEEKLY

5¢ A COPY

War, Now or Never   By Winston Churchill

Illustrations of cats dressed as people were not commonly found on old sheet music, so the charming costuming makes this late-nineteenth-century song sheet cover especially interesting. The "Cat's Galop" has no words, but the lyrics for "Cat's Duett" are all "Miau!"

Rags were the rage from 1897 to about 1917, and cats were featured on the covers of many music sheets during this era. Originally played in saloons and houses of ill repute during the late 1800s, jaunty rag melodies caught the public's fancy and became a worldwide craze. "The Black Cat Rag" was published in 1905.

"Wrigley's Black Mascot" perched atop bars of Wrigley's Scouring Soap on this change tray from the turn of the century. Miniature advertising trays like this were given free to stores and restaurants by manufacturers, to hold a customer's change after payment. Before William Wrigley, Jr., became famous for his chewing gum business, he sold soap in Chicago for his father's Philadelphia company—the Wrigley Manufacturing Company. To promote the soap and other products, such as baking powder, Wrigley tried giving away umbrellas, cookbooks, and then chewing gum free with purchases. The gum was so popular that by 1895 he had stopped selling everything but the chewing gum—and his success in that business is known the world over. The elder Wrigley's soap business continued until around 1930.

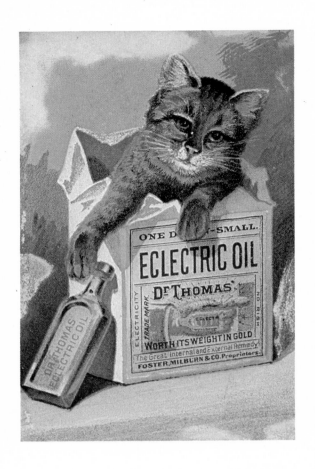

Dr. Thomas' Electric Oil Liniment was a good old-fashioned patent medicine, the kind that claimed to cure all kinds of ills. Foster, Milburn & Co. of Buffalo, New York, acquired the rights to the product—presumably from Dr. Thomas himself—in the 1880s, when the product had been on the market for about fifteen years. By the time the cat endorsement appeared on this advertising card, the Pure Food and Drug Act of 1906 was in effect. So the name of the popular liniment, which could be used both internally and externally, was changed to Dr. Thomas' *Eclectric* Oil. (After all, there really wasn't any electricity in it, despite the lightning bolts on the label.) Foster, Milburn later expanded into the prescription drug field and in 1949 became Westwood Pharmaceuticals, now a subsidiary of Bristol-Myers Company.

When Ephraim S. Wells got tired of fighting rats in the basement of his Jersey City, New Jersey, home in 1872, he developed his own rodent-elimination product. "Rough on Rats," as it was jokingly called by his wife, became an immediate commercial success. As a result, the E. S. Wells Company prospered, and other "Rough on . . ." products followed, including Rough on Corns, Bunions, Roaches, Fleas, Bed Bugs, Moths, and Ants. For years, Wells himself created all of the company's advertising—including such imaginative themes as the disappointed cats shown on this advertising card from the 1880s. Rough on Rats is the oldest U.S. registered rat-control-product trademark. It is still made, but without its original arsenic base, produced by the Brown Manufacturing Co., Le Roy, New York. The formula was revised in the late 1940s.

These packages of Household Tacks, made by the Diamond Tack
& Nail Works of Raynham, Massachusetts, put some charm on the
shelves of hardware stores more than half a century ago. Raynham
was rich in iron ore in the nineteenth century and was the site of
the first ironworks in the United States. When the railroad came
to town in 1840, many industries sprang up, because the trains
directly linked Raynham—and its iron resources—to New
England markets for the first time. One of these early
manufacturers later became the Diamond Tack & Nail Works. The
company was in business from 1909 to 1930.

maginative illustration set Black Cat Hosiery apart from the competition in turn-of-the-century magazine advertising. Dozens of different advertisements appeared in popular publications, each with black cats engaged in comical energetic activity.

Cats swam, climbed, and pranced—and were portrayed giant-size for children to cuddle. This "personality" undoubtedly helped Black Cat gain recognition—and the loyalty of magazine readers—even though the ads were generally rather small.

The Black Cat appeared silk-screened at the toe of the hosiery (made for men, women, boys, and girls) and on printed advertising, signs, and store displays. Over the years, the cat had several different looks, as shown in the accompanying photos.

The men behind the Black Cat were brothers—Charles, Willis, and Henry Cooper. In the early 1890s they left the family's knitting mill in Michigan and established the Black Cat Hosiery Company in Kenosha, Wisconsin. They also formed the Chicago-Rockford Hosiery Co., later renamed the Chicago-Kenosha Hosiery Co., to sell the hosiery to merchants nationwide.

Imagination carried over from advertising to other promotions for Black Cat. In 1899 a free Christmas book was given away to children: *The Three Black Kittens and Their Black Cat Stockings.* In 1907 merchants who carried the Black Cat brand conducted art and short story contests for children.

In 1903 two of the Coopers were killed in a fire that took hundreds of lives at the Iroquois Theater in Chicago. The remaining brother sold the hosiery business in 1913, and the famous Black Cat advertising was seen very little after that.

But Henry Cooper continued to operate a related business that the brothers had begun in 1901—the Cooper Underwear Company, located across the street from the Black Cat hosiery mill. From 1901 until 1911, Cooper underwear carried the White Cat brand name, and the trademark was a white cat that closely resembled the hosiery's black cat.

This 22″-high black cat was a three-dimensional display of the famous Black Cat Hosiery trademark.

The Black Cat trademark changed over the years—first appearing as a realistic-looking cat, then incorporating the Black Cat name, as shown on the three-foot-long metal outdoor dealer sign above.

Black cats sometimes stood for good luck in early American folklore, which may explain the appearance of the phrase on celluloid pin-back buttons. Sales through in-home gatherings are also indicated by the wording on the pin.

A charming, unique style characterized Black Cat Hosiery advertising, which could be found in many major magazines after the turn of the century. All the ads shown are from before 1910. The Black Cat trademark was imaginatively woven into the advertising, and even silk-screened on the toes of the stockings themselves.

WE GUARANTEE BLACK CAT STOCKINGS

BETTER THAN ALL OTHERS FOR WEAR

"If you like them, tell your friends—if not, tell us." For sale by most dealers. If unobtainable order from factory, 25 cents per pair. All kinds, all sizes.

CHICAGO-ROCKFORD HOSIERY COMPANY, Kenosha, Wisconsin

BLACK CAT HOSIERY

EVERY pair of Black Cat Stockings is guaranteed absolutely satisfactory, and every dealer is instructed to replace without question any pair that is defective.

This means that when you buy

Black Cat Hosiery

For Boys and Girls
Men and Women

you know positively that the hose will actually be worth the money you pay for them—the fit, the finish, the wear and the appearance are all that you expect.

The quality of the yarn, the fastness of the dyes, and the skill of the workmen make Black Cat Hosiery the most economical and satisfactory hosiery you can buy.

Ask your dealer for Style No. 15 for boys and for Style No. 10 for girls.

25c the pair

Send us 25c. for a sample pair, stating size and whether Style No. 15 or Style No. 10 is desired. For a fine dressy stocking of extra quality try Style No. 40 for boys, or Style No. 30 for girls. Write us for styles for men and women.

CHICAGO-KENOSHA HOSIERY COMPANY
900 Prairie Ave., Kenosha, Wis.

BLACK CAT TRIPLE-KNEE STOCKINGS

For Boys

25c.

a Pair

They Outwear Two Pairs of Ordinary Stockings

Triple (3-thread) knees, heels and toes, of the finest, smoothest, softest cotton yarn, Black Cat Brand, Style 15 for Boys, the strongest, most elastic and cheapest Fast Black boys' stocking in the world. Style 10 for Girls. If your dealer does not keep them, sample pair sent for

25c.

(give size), and name of dealer where you can buy again. Black Cat Stockings for men, women and children, guaranteed to give equal satisfaction.

Sample Triple Knee Sent Free

Chicago-Rockford Hosiery Company
KENOSHA, WIS.

White Cat was a complete line of men's cotton and woolen underwear. The cat symbol appeared in magazine advertising, on dealer signs, and on merchandise boxes. The advertising, however, emphasized illustrations of the underwear rather than the cat, and lacked the creative flair of early Black Cat ads.

In 1908 the company was known as the largest men's underwear factory in the United States and as the "Home of the White Cat." Unfortunately, the White Cat name, and then the cat image, was dropped within a few years. The focus shifted to the "Kenosha Klosed Krotch Union Suit"—a unique crossed panel design that reduced the bulkiness of men's underwear and revolutionized the undergarment business.

This achievement assured longevity for the Cooper Underwear Company, which, many years later, also developed "jockey shorts." In 1971 the company officially became Jockey International, Inc.

The White Cat trademark appeared on Cooper Underwear Company boxes (*detail of lid shown at right*), on signs, and in magazine advertising prior to 1911. Pocket mirrors were popular advertising items given free by the company's salesmen to retail merchants and their customers. The oval mirror shows the company's focus on the White Cat brand name and trademark in the early 1900s. The round mirror shows the later emphasis changing to an illustration of the new "Klosed Krotch" product.

The life-size likeness of "Tom Hidden" makes this paper advertising sign from the Otis Hidden Company a very unusual promotional item. The cat must have also appeared on the Hidden brand of window shades, from the reference in the lower left corner. The Louisville, Kentucky, company was 100 years old when it was sold in 1964. The sign is from the early 1900s and is just under two feet tall.

"A Wedding in Catland" is a puzzle that advertised Hood's Sarsaparilla and Hood's Pills, popular nineteenth-century patent medicines. The sarsaparilla was a tonic made of roots, barks, and herbs; it allegedly purified the blood, increased the appetite, and restored vitality. The pills, sold as a cathartic and liver medicine, were said to be made of "pure vegetable." The wedding scene was illustrated by Louis Wain, an artist who is noted for his cat drawings that were made into prints, postcards, and bookplates around the turn of the century. The C. I. Hood Co. of Lowell, Massachusetts, included this 14½″ x 10″ puzzle in a series of "Puzzles for Rainy Days"—with an advertising message on the back—in the early 1900s. Warner-Lambert Pharmaceuticals Co. now owns the Hood name, but the products have not been sold for many years.

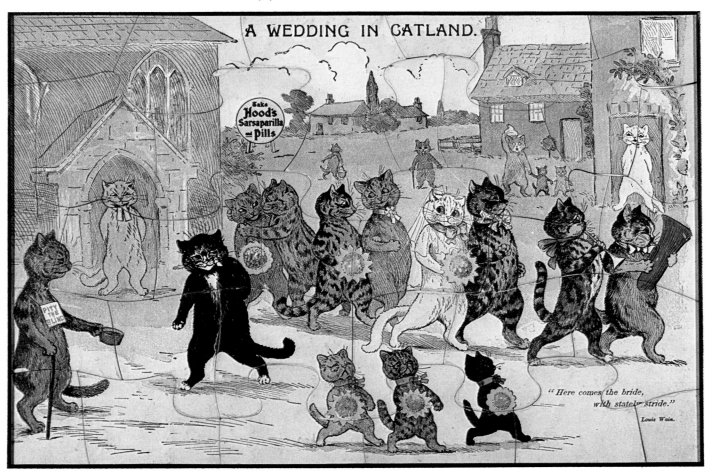

This early die-cut sign probably hung on a shoe repair shop wall. It is three-dimensional, with raised detail and lettering, and measures 13½″ x 10″. The colorful advertisement is from a theater program booklet.

For decades, a lighted electric clock more than a foot in diameter was a familiar sight in shoe repair shops across the United States. This example is from around 1948. Shop owners say it was given to them with the purchase of large amounts of rubber goods.

he Cat's Paw name has been prominent in shoe repair shops since the early 1900s. The Massachusetts Chemical Company of Boston registered the name as a rubber-footwear trademark; within a year the mark was also extended to rubber heels and soles—the products for which Cat's Paw is famous.

Because cats are surefooted and agile, the cat was an excellent choice as a footwear symbol. First used as a full-body silhouette with tail held high in the air, the cat later changed to the modern close-up head-and-shoulders version. Its raised paw is a clever illustration of the Cat's Paw name.

The cat has always been an important part of Cat's Paw advertising and was used in magazine ads, posters, and packages under the Foster Rubber Company name. It was even embossed on early versions of the rubber soles. When the high-tailed symbol was in use, it alternately faced left or right—whichever looked best in the advertising.

The Cat's Paw brand and cat live on as the property of the Biltright Corporation, Chelsea, Massachusetts, and shoe repair shops still stock Cat's Paw products—just as they have for the better part of this century.

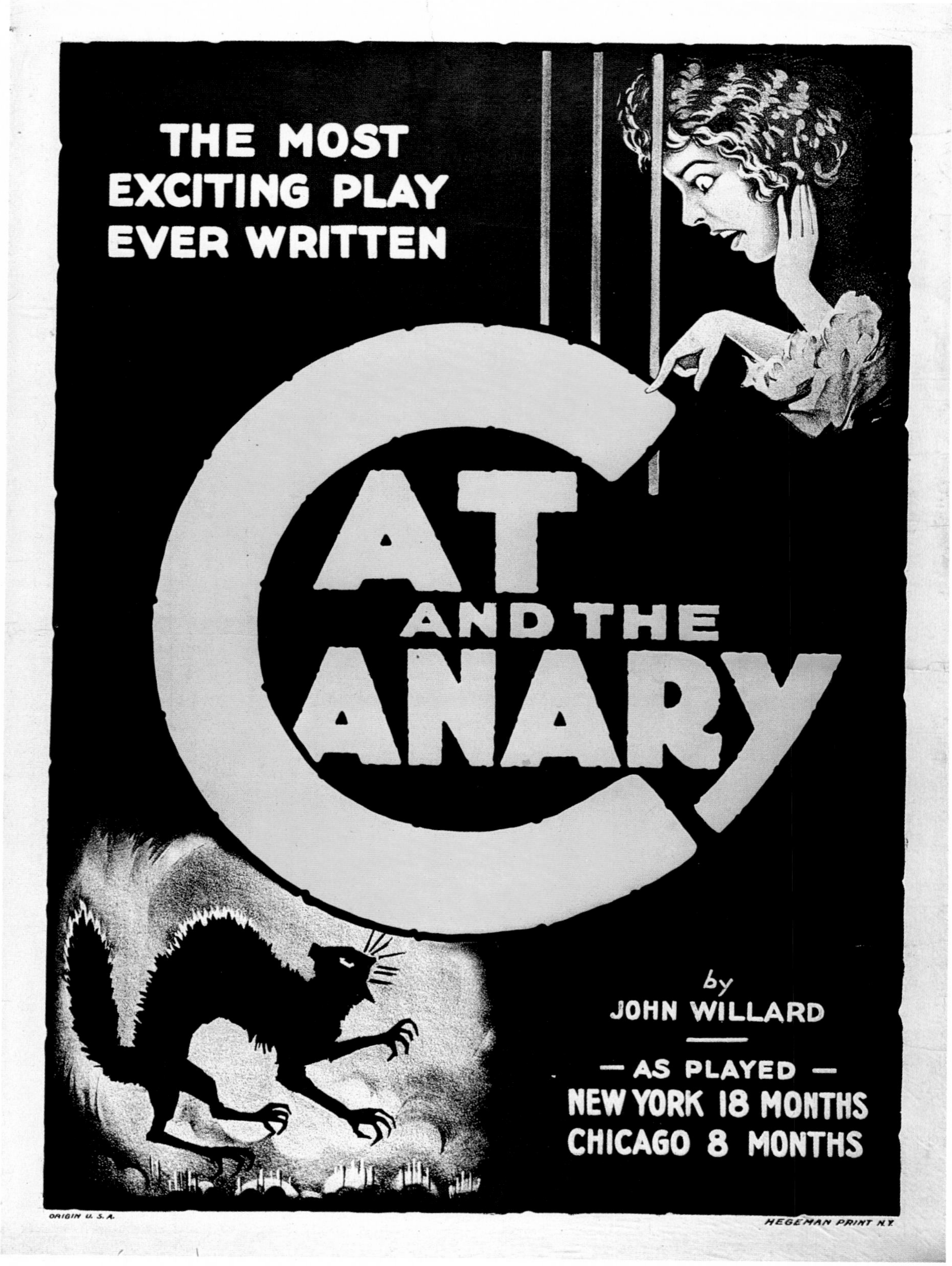

THE MOST
EXCITING PLAY
EVER WRITTEN

CAT AND THE CANARY

by
JOHN WILLARD

— AS PLAYED —
NEW YORK 18 MONTHS
CHICAGO 8 MONTHS

ORIGIN U.S.A.

HEGEMAN PRINT N.Y.

A review of the play *Cat and the Canary* (1922) called it "a sensational tale of noisy and intimidating woes and harrowing scenes." The three-act mystery by John Willard captivated audiences in New York and Chicago during the 1920s and is still occasionally produced by local theater companies. In 1927, this story of a young heiress—the victim of macabre attempts by one of her relatives to drive her insane in order to acquire her fortune—was made into a silent movie. Although a cat appeared on the theater poster shown here, the title was purely symbolic. It compared the innocent heiress to a helpless caged canary, preyed upon by a cat. Actual poster size is 28″ x 20″.

A pet may be a person's best friend—and to lose a pet can be heartbreaking. "Has Anybody Seen My Kitty," published in 1922, is a song about two neighbors searching for their lost cats. Photographs of singers and bands often appeared on sheet music covers from this era; a photo encircled by a cat, however, is unusually eye-catching.

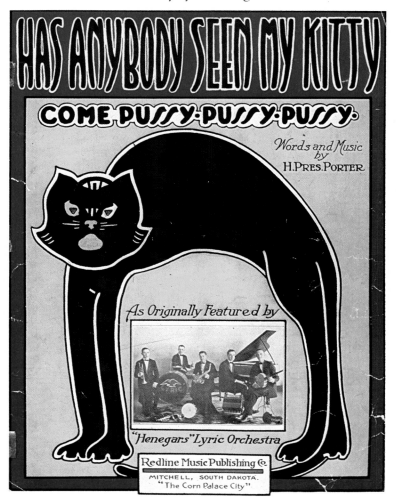

"For Kiddies Not Kitties"

WAXTITE
THE PERFECT PACKAGE

Kellogg's
TOASTED
CORN
FLAKES
THE ORIGINAL HAS THIS SIGNATURE
W. K. Kellogg
KELLOGG TOASTED CORN FLAKE CO.
BATTLE CREEK, MICH.
The sweetheart of the corn

BETTER corn flakes than Kellogg's when just made are not possible. The WAXTITE package insures your getting Kellogg's just as they are when we make them, fresh, crisp and tasty. WAXTITE is perfect protection to ready-to-serve food.

Look for this signature

W. K. Kellogg

A delightful headline and illustration helped the Kellogg Toasted Corn Flake Company of Battle Creek, Michigan, promote its cereal in this 1914 magazine advertisement. The signature of W. K. Kellogg, the company founder, appeared on the package and in advertising of this era to help distinguish Kellogg's Corn Flakes®—originally developed by Kellogg and his brother in 1898—from a large number of competitors who copied the product. "Crinkle the Cat" was one of a series of Colorful Cloth Dolls offered by the company in the mid-1930s. Customers received the sew-it-yourself dolls for sending in one package top from Kellogg's Wheat Krispies® and ten cents. Unassembled, the Crinkle preprinted cloth pattern (dated 1935) measured 17″ x 13″. The Kellogg Company is still producing the cereals that breakfast lovers have enjoyed for generations.

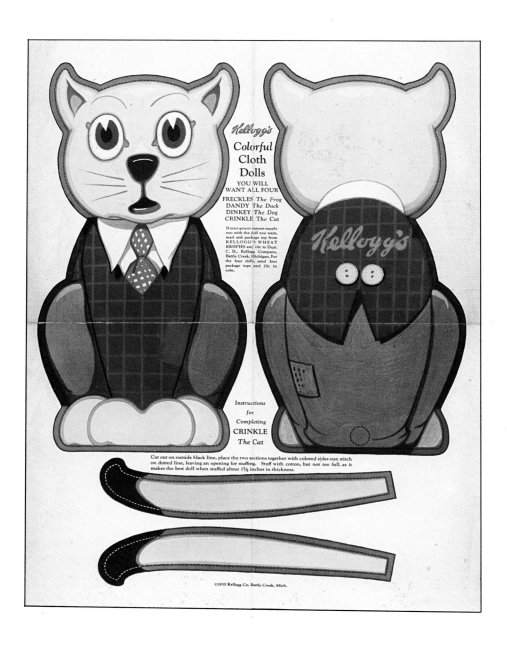

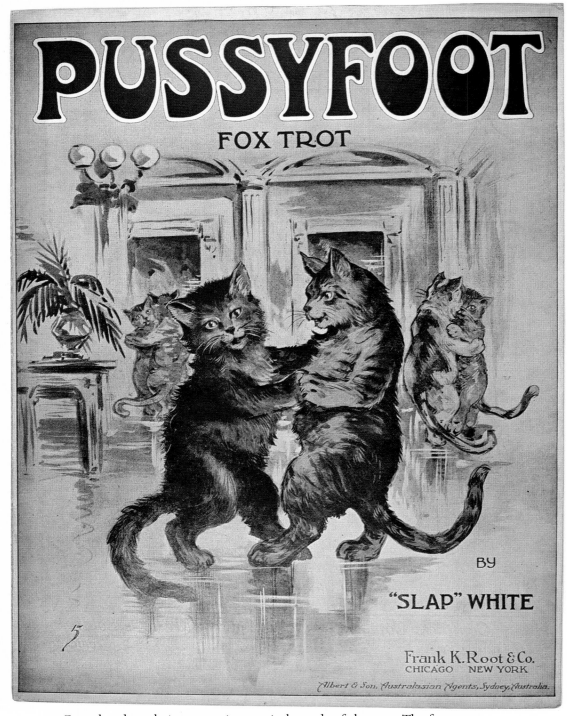

Cats played a role in promoting musical trends of the past. The fox-trot came onto the dance scene around 1915, and the "Pussyfoot Fox Trot" showed two cats engaged in the new dance on the cover of the music sheet. Another edition of this music was published the same year with the same cover illustration, but it was titled "Pussyfoot Prance"—probably because the publisher was uncertain how popular the fox-trot would be!

"The Pussy Cat Rag," published in 1913, was a lively composition characteristic of pre–World War I ragtime music. Its lyrics are a tale of woe told by a man whose sister has late-night rendezvous with alley cats.

ANOTHER "HIT" BY THE WRITERS OF "WHAT D'YE MEAN YOU LOST YER DOG"

THE PUSSY CAT RAG

(KITTY, KITTY, KITTY, KITTY)

WORDS BY
THOS. S. ALLEN

MUSIC BY
JOSEPH M. DALY
AND THOS. S. ALLEN

Daly
MUSIC PUBLISHER
BOSTON, MASS.

This Honest Scrap chewing tobacco sign, which measures 30″ x 22″, came already framed, to be hung in tobacco shops near the turn of the century. The testy dog and cat were also lithographed on large tin counter-top display bins for customers' self-service selection. In 1910, the story of the fictitious scrap between the pair was told in an illustrated booklet given away to customers (the cat won!). When Lorillard, America's oldest tobacco company, offered this product, chewing tobacco had already seen a century of popularity in the United States.

This charming 12½″-tall counter sign from the late 1800s advertised Boraxine soap powder, made by J. D. Larkin & Co., Buffalo, New York. The Larkin name is best known for its innovative offering of free gifts to customers who purchased Larkin products—such as paint, soap, foods, and pharmaceuticals. Illustrated Larkin catalogs from 1893 to the mid-1930s included a wide array of household goods and furnishings from which customers could select the items they had earned. John D. Larkin's company was also the first to pack free gifts *inside* product packages. Small cards printed with illustrations of children, animals, flowers, and other themes were included in Boraxine packages as a buying incentive. Despite its creativity, the Larkin company fell upon hard times during the Depression years and finally went out of business around 1940.

If the picture could make you smile, perhaps you would remember the product. Such logic was often used in designing early advertising; the situation illustrated by a cat on the Maple City Self Washing Soap advertising card is a good example. Maple City laundry and toilet soap was first made around 1880. The manufacturer, Maple City Soap Works, was purchased in 1908 by the Procter & Gamble Co. of Cincinnati, Ohio—already quite successful with its Ivory brand.

Dr. A. C. Daniels knew cats had a centuries-old attraction to catnip. So he designed and patented a unique exercise toy in 1907—a smooth, hollow wooden ball that could be filled with dry catnip leaves. This figural store display sign, dated 1907 and measuring 19″ x 11″, promoted both the ball and his special brand of catnip. With the ball's success, a catnip mouse was soon introduced, and business started booming for Daniels's small Boston veterinary supply business, which he had begun in 1878. Pet shops still carry the catnip balls, made by the current company, Dr. A. C. Daniels, Inc. The package is virtually the same as it was when it was introduced almost eighty years ago.

The Ultra Shoe kitten was featured in a series of magazine advertisements at the turn of the century. The artist revealed his understanding of cats when he drew the kitten peering out from behind the popular shoe styles—or snuggling against them—with surprising realism. A 1900 ad told readers to "See What Kittie Does Next!"—an enticement to watch for more kitten antics in future ads. The shoes "Fit for a Queen" were sold in the United States, Canada, and the West Indies until the Moore-Shafer Shoe Company, founded in 1888, went out of business in 1927.

The Fisk Tire Company of Chicopee Falls, Massachusetts, captured readers' attention by using a protective mother cat in this 1926 advertisement from *Country Life* magazine. Fisk's famous sleepy boy logo and their "Time to Re-tire" slogan were ingeniously incorporated into the ad. Fisk was purchased by the U.S. Rubber Co. (now Uniroyal, Inc.) in 1937.

Another type of cat was featured by the Ethyl Gasoline Corp. in 1929–31 magazine advertising. Ethyl, a tetraethyl lead gasoline additive that prevents engine knock, was discovered by General Motors researchers in 1924 and manufactured by Standard Oil of New Jersey. The Ethyl Gasoline Corp. was a sales company jointly created to market Ethyl to oil refiners. The Abermarle Paper Co. purchased the Ethyl Gasoline Corp. in 1962, and Ethyl can still be found in many modern gasolines.

n advertising writer who also enjoyed writing short stories began publishing *The Black Cat* magazine in October 1895. Herman D. Umbstaetter gambled that America would buy a monthly publication devoted entirely to short fiction by amateur writers—and he was right. Within three years, *The Black Cat* claimed a circulation of nearly 200,000 per month.

For the first couple of years, each cover portrayed a black cat in a different eye-catching scene. They were charming fantasies that costumed the cat as an artist, minstrel, bicycle rider, ballerina, court jester—even with butterfly wings.

These colorful Art Nouveau creations came from the imagination of Nelly Littlehale Umbstaetter, the publisher's wife. In addition to their use on covers, the drawings were offered to readers as a series of prints for one dollar with a new subscription (fifty cents per year). Some of the cover images were also designed into tiny fashionable stickpins that were offered for sale to subscribers.

Black cats decorated the stories in each issue as well—entwined with the first letter of each story. Several examples can be seen in the text of this book. Other original cat drawings were placed at the end of the stories; an example is on page 96.

The *New York Herald* once called *The Black Cat* magazine "the cat that captured the country" because of its popularity. Hopeful writers were encouraged to enter stories in writing contests Umbstaetter promoted. The prizes, in addition to publication in the magazine, included thousands of dollars in prize money and even a trip around the world. Some of the well-known writers who credited *The Black Cat* with their initial success were Jack London and Octavus Roy Cohen.

Over the years, *The Black Cat* changed, just as the nation did. The intricate covers were switched to plainer, more geometric backgrounds showing only the cat's face. The price of the magazine, originally a "nickel monthly," was increased to twenty cents by 1920. Umbstaetter died in 1913, and the succession of editors and owners who followed him could never recapture the spirit of the earlier issues. Its circulation steadily declined, and *The Black Cat* finally ceased publication in 1923.

The black cat that was featured on covers of *The Black Cat* magazine was shown dressed up and in interesting active roles, as shown above. The detail at the top of page 52 is from the cover of the December 1898 issue—after the magazine stopped using full-figurals on the covers.

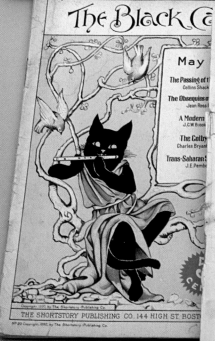

This advertisement for Sapolio soap was specifically tailored to fit into the style and theme of *The Black Cat* magazine, in which it appeared around 1896. Sapolio was first made by the Enoch Morgan's Sons company in 1869 and was the first scouring powder produced in the United States.

Subscribers to *The Black Cat* magazine saw a variety of colorful covers during a subscription year. Those shown at left were published between 1895 and 1904.

hessie is probably the most famous cat in American advertising history. Known as "America's Sleepheart," the tabby kitten first promoted the Chesapeake and Ohio Railway in a September 1933 advertisement in *Fortune* magazine.

"Sleep like a Kitten" was Chessie's official slogan, and she has always been shown as she was first portrayed by the Viennese artist Guido Gruenwald in 1933. A company official liked the drawing when it appeared in a New York newspaper, and the C & O Railway acquired the rights to Chessie shortly thereafter.

A family of two kittens was added on the 1935 Chessie calendar—the second calendar in what was to be an annual tradition for several decades. For Father's Day 1937, a "husband"—called Peake—was introduced, largely in response to questions from the public about the identity of the kittens' father.

Chessie was so popular that everything on board the trains, from dining-car china to towels, was soon imprinted with the kitten symbol. The company began to merchandise Chessie souvenirs in 1948.

Chessie System Railroads now owns the Chessie trademark. A 1963 merger created the company from the former C & O and Baltimore and Ohio railways. After over fifty years of riding the rails, Chessie can be seen today stenciled larger than life on Chessie System locomotives and freight cars; passenger service is no longer offered.

Right page: Chessie looked particularly sweet in this 1936 magazine advertisement, three years after she first appeared as the Chesapeake and Ohio Railway mascot. *Left:* Peake, Chessie's "husband," was introduced to Chessie's admiring public in this 1937 magazine advertisement. *Above:* Chessie promotional souvenir items include matchbooks, a pin-back lapel button, playing cards, and a key chain.

56

The cat on this unusual two-sided advertising card helped emphasize how much babies liked Lactated Food, a formula Wells, Richardson & Co. of Burlington, Vermont, claimed could save babies' lives because it tasted so good it could coax sick infants to eat. Among Wells, Richardson's best sellers were also Diamond Dyes for fabrics and some unusual over-the-counter medicines—such as Kidney-Wort Preparation, which treated a variety of ailments, and Paine's Celery Compound, said to have contained a high concentration of alcohol and a generous dash of cocaine. After the Pure Food and Drug Act of 1906 required disclosure of product contents on the package labels, the questionable-medicine market sharply declined, and along with it, Wells, Richardson's sales. The company was sold in 1922 to Sterling Drug, Inc., a New York–based pharmaceutical company. Lactated food is no longer produced.

In the 1880s and '90s, cats appeared on several creatively illustrated advertising cards for Willimantic, the first American-made cotton sewing machine thread. When Willimantic was introduced in 1856, Scottish thread was the major competition. Salesmen for the imported brands told people that the U.S. climate was so dry that a high-quality cotton thread could not be produced here; they said static electricity would cause the thread to break during the manufacturing process. But the Willimantic Linen Company ingeniously planted flowers in window boxes at the thread mill and in nearby yards to create moisture in the air—and the dryness problem at the factory was overcome! As early as the 1890s, the company had earned a reputation as a progressive employer that offered its two thousand workers extensive benefits. Willimantic continues as the American Thread Co., still located in Willimantic, Connecticut.

What are these Babies after?

This Carter's Ink bottle is from the early 1940s. The prancing felines on the label were seen throughout the 1940s and, somewhat updated, into the 1950s. The bottle was made to fit into Carter's desk sets—a design accomplishment that eliminated the need to pour the ink from its bottle into a separate desk-top container. The 138-year-old company stopped producing writing inks in 1958. Today, the Dennison Manufacturing Co. (formerly the Dennison-Carter Co.) produces stationery products.

Before the days of ballpoint pens, ink blotters were necessary desk-top accessories that also could keep the advertising message for a product—and its dealers—always in view. The L. H. Thomas Company of Chicago produced this ink blotter, which prominently showed a cat as the symbol for Thomas' Inks, around 1900. The slogan "Ask For Me" encouraged customers to ask for "the ink with the cat on the bottle" when selecting their writing fluid. The Thomas Company (1885–1931) was acquired by the Sanford Corporation, but Thomas' Inks are no longer made.

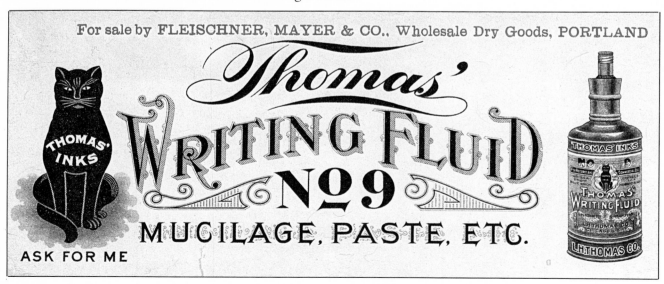

"Carter's Kittens" helped sell Carter's Ink from 1941 to 1957 in a series of magazine advertisements showing a mother cat and her multicolored family. Illustrations included a nine-kitten softball team and a kitten footrace, accompanied by the "Carter's Ink has 9 'dyes'" slogan. Prints of the colorful kitten illustrations were offered as free promotional giveaways to the public, as were color-it-yourself kitten outlines—to be colored with Carter's Ink, of course. This advertisement appeared in 1943.

The allure of the unknown and everyone's natural curiosity made The Black Cat Fortune Telling Game a popular offering by Parker Brothers for four decades. First introduced in 1897, the game offers to tell the past, present, and future for all players, give advice of a general nature and on "matters of the heart," and warn against danger. On the back of each card, groups of words are arranged in twenty-four rows. When randomly drawn cards are matched against each other, the rows line up to form complete sentences. Since legends and folklore link cats with both good luck and superstition, it is not hard to understand why Parker Brothers chose the cat as this game's artistic focus. The edition pictured here is from before 1901.

A gentle kitten brought attention to the soothing properties of Packer's Tar Soap in this quaint magazine advertisement from 1899. The soap was scented with pine tar, and the Packer Manufacturing Company of New York built a strong reputation for it as a medicinal aid through extensive advertising campaigns. Ads claimed that Packer's soap could cure baldness and skin disorders, among other ailments. The kitten ad was used for almost a decade. Cooper Laboratories continues to produce the soap today.

THE BLACK CAT Fortune Telling GAME
Parker Brothers
SALEM, MASS. U.S.A.
COPYRIGHT 1897

♠ The Present

♣ DANGER!

♦ The Future

♥ Love Matters

The Past

♦ General Advice

This beautiful advertisement appeared in *Ladies' Home Journal* in December 1918. It was one of a series from the Allen B. Wrisley Company of Chicago that linked beauty and Olivilo Soap with popular folklore; another in the campaign featured the Bluebird of Happiness. The Olivilo name indicated that olive oil, a moisturizing agent, was one of its ingredients. In 1961, the Wrisley Company became part of Purex Corporation. Olivilo is no longer produced.

The Bon Ami Company frequently used cats in turn-of-the-century advertising to illustrate its famous "Can't Scratch" theme. The product that is so well known today almost escaped discovery a century ago. Purely by accident, a New England soapmaker—John T. Robertson—discovered that feldspar (Bon Ami's main ingredient) could polish various surfaces. He was shoveling feldspar waste—which is a byproduct of quartz created in the soap-making process—when he noticed his old shovel had become shiny. He followed a friend's suggestion and gave the new discovery a fancy-sounding French name in 1886. Bon Ami is still produced; it is now a product of the Faultless Starch Company.

Before the B. F. Goodrich Company made automobile tires, it made other rubber products, including fire hoses, bicycle tires, and boots. This seventeen-inch-wide paper advertising sign from around 1920 humorously demonstrated that with Goodrich rubbers even cats—notorious for their dislike of water—could stay happy and dry in the rain. The sign was used inside shops or on dealers' windows. Goodrich, of course, still produces tires, but not the rubbers.

Nursery rhymes provided the theme for a 1923 magazine advertising campaign for Rogers Silverplate flatware. In this example, which appeared in *Ladies' Home Journal,* Rogers's durable tableware was said to survive like a cat—through the legendary nine lives. The Wm. Rogers & Son trademark dates back to 1866; in 1898 the Connecticut company became part of the International Silver Company, which is still in business.

*"Kitty," said Miss Prue with pride,
"On this please meditate:
Your nine lives, if multiplied,
Would not outlast this silverplate."*

THE cat gained its widespread reputation for many lives by demonstrating that it could withstand hard knocks. Wm. Rogers & Son silverplate has built up a reputation for long and constant wear by more than 50 years of satisfactory service. Now, added to that reputation is the unlimited guarantee that goes with each piece of Wm. Rogers & Son silverplate.

Therefore, when you wish to buy silverplate either for a present or your own use, ask your dealer for Wm. Rogers & Son ware.

Wm. Rogers & Son Silverplate

MAYFAIR PATTERN
Medium Forks ~ ~ $3.50 per ½ doz.
Medium Knives ~ ~ $9.00 per ½ doz.
(Hollow Handle)
Medium Knives ~ ~ $3.25 per ½ doz.
(Solid Handle)
Teaspoons ~ ~ ~ ~ $1.25 per ½ doz.

Made and Guaranteed by
Wm. Rogers Mfg. Co. Meriden, Conn.
Succeeded by

INTERNATIONAL SILVER CO.

Also made in Canada by
Wm. Rogers Mfg. Co. Limited
Niagara Falls, Ont.

"Old Tom" is the generic nickname for a type of sweetened gin popular in the middle to late 1880s. Many different companies produced Old Tom Gins, and they far outsold "dry" gins worldwide until about 1920. No one is sure how Old Tom acquired its name, but the most popular theories say it was to honor a man who first distilled sweetened gin more than two hundred years ago; to immortalize an eighteenth-century bootlegger; or to remember a special cat. The two Victorian-era bottle labels shown above most likely represented different Old Tom varieties made by different distillers.

Black cats have often lent their names to food, drink, and restaurants. The shaped 6½″-high menu shown is from The Black Cat restaurant, located on West Broadway in New York City in the 1920s. At the time the menu was used, customers could order a club sandwich for only eighty cents and filet mignon for a dollar and a half. Black Cat Bitter Sweet Chocolates were made by the A. G. Morse Candy Company, Chicago. Morse also produced a "Cat's Meow" brand, no doubt to capitalize on the popular slang term, in the 1920s. Black Cat Bitter Sweet Chocolates—packed in the one-pound box shown—were sold in the 1930s.

35 Cents
$3.50 a Year

THE MAGAZINE FOR PLAYGOERS.

SEPTEMBER, 1913
VOL. XVIII. NO. 151

THE THEATRE

(TITLE REG. U. S. PAT. OFF.)

Miss MARY PICKFORD

The Theatre Magazine Co.,
8-10-12-14 West 38th St. N.Y.

Mary Pickford posed with a cat for this cover of *The Theatre* magazine in September 1913. Calling itself "The Magazine for Playgoers," *The Theatre* published reviews and articles by prominent critics, actors, and other important people in the theater business from 1900 to 1931. Mary Pickford was already a well-known stage actress and had starred in two silent films by the time this portrait appeared.

A series of cartoon-animal advertising cards promoted New Home Sewing Machines between 1877 and 1882. In addition to the cats, lions were also shown using a New Home Sewing Machine. Another card pictured a fox—machine-mending his torn tail. The first U.S. patent for a straight-stitch home sewing machine was issued in 1848, and by the time this card was made, well over a half a million such machines were in use. The New Home Sewing Machine Company, now located in New Jersey, is the second largest manufacturer of sewing machines in the world, and is a subsidiary of the Janome Sewing Machine Company of Tokyo.

A black cat was the trademark used on spools of ribbon imported by Corbett Brothers, New York City, for use in the millinery industry. Silk, grosgrain, and especially their Black Cat brand of velvet ribbons accented many stylish outfits in the early twentieth century. After World War II, however, it became increasingly difficult to buy imported ribbon, and as hats also declined in fashion, many competitor companies dropped out of sight. In the early 1950s, Corbett Brothers, too, went out of business.

The Art Nouveau illustration in this striking magazine advertisement from 1900 contrasts twelve black cats with one white cat at center stage. Whether it is a slap at competition in the soap business—perhaps showing envy of Procter & Gamble's success—or simply a statement about Ivory's purity and cleaning power is unknown. So appealing was this illustration that the company offered a print of it in exchange for ten Ivory wrappers. Procter & Gamble—founded in Cincinnati in 1837—introduced the still-popular Ivory brand in 1879.

IVORY SOAP 99 44/100 PER CENT PURE

ENVY

IT FLOATS

Posing prettily, the fluffy feline on the July 1928 cover of *People's Home Journal,* a magazine for women begun in 1885, asked only to be admired. It is an "artistic" style that was used by many types of magazines over the years—strictly entertaining and without substance. The March 27, 1883, *Harper's Young People* cover, in contrast, told a story with its illustration. One of the many magazines produced by the famous Harper family, this magazine had the reputation of being an intellectual publication for children. Both of these magazines have disappeared from circulation—the last issue of *People's Home Journal* was printed in 1929; *Harper's Young People* was discontinued in 1899.

The unusual caricature on this *Puck* magazine cover was really part of a political cartoon. *Puck* was a controversial satirical weekly, published from 1877 to 1918, that poked fun at politics, religion, and society in general. The cat represented Ulysses S. Grant, who at the time of this issue (February 18, 1880) had already served two terms as the eighteenth president of the United States. The cartoon was drawn by Joseph Keppler, one of the founders of *Puck.* It depicted Grant's quest for a third term of office. (He didn't make it—he lost the 1880 Republican nomination to James Garfield.)

WILL THE CAT DO IT?

A black cat named "Tom" was used by
Ruhe Bros. & Co. of Allentown,
Pennsylvania, to represent "Mr. Thomas"
cigars (ca. 1894). This miniature
lithographed tray (which held change after a
customer sale) helped promote "Mr.
Thomas" cigars by keeping the name in
view on a dealer's counter top. The tray is
shown actual size.

The embossed "Our Kitties" cigar box label (ca. 1910–20) was produced by a lithographic printing method that required each color to be applied by a separate plate, or stone. Some of the labels produced from the 1880s to about 1920 were of such an intricate design that their printing required up to twenty-two different stones. Embossing (raised lettering or figures pressed into the paper from the opposite side) was first used in the 1890s. The cats honored by the "Our Kitties" label and cigar bands are representative of beloved pets everywhere.

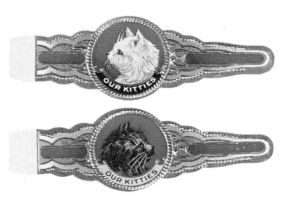

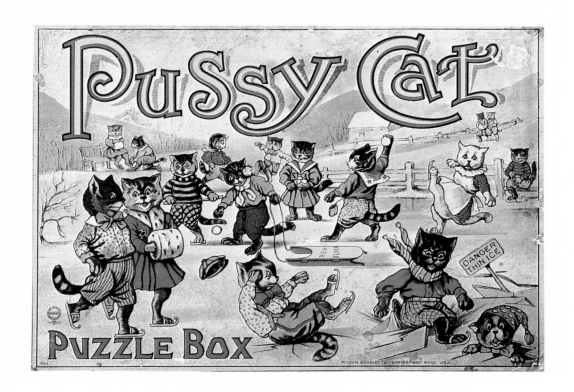

The Pussy Cat Puzzle Box made by the Milton Bradley Company of Springfield, Massachusetts, contained three jigsaw puzzles and dates back to around 1900. The puzzle designs had charming themes—cats attending a fancy banquet dinner, kittens playing after school, and ice-skating cats—shown on the box cover. Both the box lid and the assembled puzzles measured 18¼" x 12½". The Old Maid Board Game from Parker Brothers, of Salem, Massachusetts (ca. 1900–1919), was a spoof of romantic chance that challenged up to four players to land a marker on the heart designated "Yes," while avoiding the "No" heart. The bottom of the box served as the game board, and players spun an indicator to determine if they "won" the heart or were "rejected." The game box lid for this edition of the game measures 8" x 13". Both companies are still producing games in the New England towns of their founding.

The cat on this two-foot-high metal sign is standing on a Rex Flintkote roof made by the J. A. & W. Bird & Co. of Boston. Rex Flintkote Roofing was produced in prerolled, ready-to-use sheets. Advertising from 1905 to 1908 said Flintkote Roofing was easier to install than any other type of roofing. Its durable wool-felt construction was described as better than tin or combination tar-and-gravel roofs because it was "absolutely resistant" to fire, water, snow, heat, cold, and wear. The boy in the trademark is shown holding a roll of the roofing. The cat design also appeared on celluloid pin-back advertising buttons given away to dealers who carried the brand and to their customers. The modern Flintkote Company, successor to the Bird Company, produces building supplies.

LePage's Glue has been made for over a hundred years. The cartoon scene on the box label below shows how cats helped "demonstrate" the product in early advertising. The box is from the mid-1880s, when the Russia Cement Company of Gloucester, Massachusetts, produced the glue. Paper labels inside describe medals of excellence awarded the product in international competition, and say it was proclaimed "the strongest adhesive known" at a German exhibition in 1880. Today, LePage's Glue is made by LePage's Incorporated, owned by the Papercraft Corporation.

"Kitten on the Keys" was a novelty piano solo published in 1921. Its fast, intricate melody was produced on player piano rolls and phonograph records as well as sheet music. Words were added in 1922, proclaiming that "Anybody listenin' can't help whistlin' 'Kitten on the Keys.'" The song proved to be quite popular, and its success was the high point in composer Edward "Zez" Confrey's career.

With a little imagination, the troupe of cats on the cover of the "Black Cat Patrol" sheet music would almost spring to life as the brisk melody was played. The music was published in 1896.

Corticelli Silk

Too Strong To Break

Send for this handy Corticelli Sewing Stand to hold eight Spools

Does Not Knot

he Corticelli Kitten is one of the most interesting examples of cats in advertising. The Belding Heminway Company, Inc.—makers of Corticelli silk, cotton, and synthetic sewing threads—owns the group of playful feline designs, which has played an important role in promoting the Corticelli name since the turn of the century.

Corticelli actually dates back to 1832, when the Northampton Silk Company was founded in Massachusetts. Thirteen years later, Samuel Hill purchased the business and renamed it The Nonotuck Silk Company. Then, as now, certain imports were considered status symbols. Italy was known for its silk, so Hill capitalized upon this foreign mystique by creating an Italian-sounding brand name for the Nonotuck products: Corticelli.

Kittens were introduced into Corticelli advertising around 1900. In fact, "kitten ads" could be found in almost every popular women's magazine of the day for the first couple of decades of the twentieth century.

Sewing was on the upswing, and women loved the kitten. They showed it by buying Corticelli products—including silk sewing thread; embroidery, crochet, and tatting thread; purse "twist"; and silk fabric—in such numbers that the company became an industry leader. In 1922, the company officially became the Corticelli Silk Company to take advantage of the phenomenal consumer recognition of the Corticelli name.

In addition to magazine advertising, the kitten design appeared on signs, packages and spools of thread, store display cabinets, labels, instruction booklets showing how to make fashionable clothing and accessories with Corticelli products, and countless advertising items given free to customers.

In 1911, a prominent artist, Ben Austrian, immortalized the kitten on canvas; a facsimile of his oil painting hangs in the Belding Heminway corporate headquarters in New York today. (The original painting disappeared some years ago and, despite an all-out search, was never recovered.)

Left: This full-page advertisement for Corticelli silk thread was one of the most colorful—and beautiful—ads found in women's magazines in 1912. *Right:* The kitten painted by Ben Austrian was reproduced on this advertising postcard, sent to customers by shops carrying the Corticelli brand, around 1913. The use of cats on the back showed exceptional design creativity.

Corticelli SPOOL SEWING SILK

HOW provoking it is to use silk that's constantly breaking. Use Corticelli Spool Silk and sewing will become a pleasure. For dressmaking and family sewing it has no equal. Any sewing for which you would use silk at all deserves good silk. As Corticelli costs you no more than poor silk, why not ask for the best and then see that you get it?

Corticelli

Corticelli SPOOL SILK & EMBROIDERY WASH SILK

Highest Award
AT ALL EXPOSITIONS
There is

No Silk So Smooth
No Silk So Long
No Silk So Strong

As

Corticelli

It is Economy

to buy silk you can depend upon. No silk is so strong, even, smooth, and perfect in finish as the celebrated Corticelli, made in the largest silk thread works in the world. All sizes and colors for sewing, stitching, crocheting, and art needle-work

Corticelli Silk

Your new dress will wear longer and give greater satisfaction if good strong silk like Corticelli is used in the making. As Corticelli costs no more than poor silk, be sure that "Corticelli" is stamped on each spool you buy. Ask for Corticelli, the Kitten Silk, and refuse all others.

Corticelli Silk Mills
FLORENCE, MASS.

Corticelli Silk

smooth, elastic and strong, and its

Corticelli Silk is Pure!

Everybody knows "Corticelli" is the best silk for sewing, stitching, crocheting, art needlework, Mountmellick and Hardanger embroidery. Send 4c. in stamps for our booklet, "Lessons in Embroidery." Address Corticelli Silk Mills, 77 Nonotuck St., Florence, Mass.

Corticelli SPOOL SILK

CORTICELLI is the Dressmakers' Favorite silk. It is smooth, even, and strong

Corticelli Silk

Perhaps you cannot tell the difference by *looking* at the silk, but you will know at once by *trying* it that Corticelli Silk runs smoother and is stronger than other kinds. You consult your own best interest every time you *insist* on getting Corticelli. For hand or machine sewing it has no equal. **If You Are Not Your Own Dressmaker** see to it that whoever does your sewing uses Corticelli Silk when making your new dress. As Corticelli Silk costs no more than poor silk, be sure that "Corticelli" is stamped on each spool you buy. Ask for Corticelli, the Kitten Silk.

Corticelli Silk Mills
28 Nonotuck St.
Florence, Mass

Corticelli Silk
WEARS LONGEST AND HOLDS STRONGEST

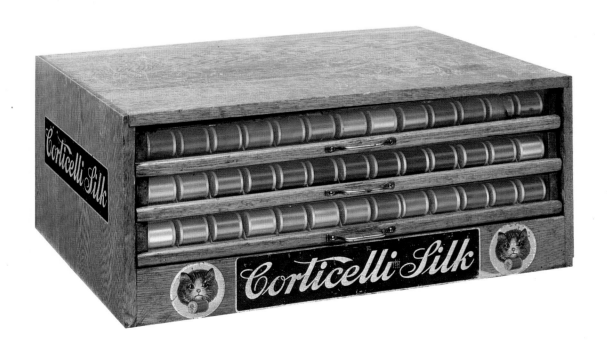

Left: Magazine advertising repeatedly brought the Corticelli kitten into American homes. The examples shown appeared in magazines such as *Ladies' Home Journal, The Delineator,* and *McCall's* in the early 1900s and show the diversity of styles used. The Corticelli package label (*right*) and the thread spool cabinet (*below*) were familiar sights to shoppers during the early years of this century. The three-drawer cabinet is made of oak, measures 20½″ x 15½″ x 8½″, and was designed to show the variety of Corticelli thread colors through its glass panels. It can hold 507 spools of thread.

The kitten also made advertising history high above New York City in the early 1900s. A huge animated electric kitten sign was placed atop an office building, showing the kitten playing with Corticelli thread. The sight drew crowds in the streets far below. It was the first such advertising sign to appear above Times Square and one of the first signs of this type in the world.

By 1901, when Corticelli won a gold medal at the Pan-American Exposition in Buffalo, the company had already received nearly forty other first-prize awards at fairs and competitions. In the early 1900s, customers could write to the company for a complimentary souvenir box of Corticelli silk cocoons—the same as were given to the public at the company's Pan-American booth.

The current Belding Heminway Company, Inc., was created by a consolidation with two other large silk manufacturing firms. The Heminway and Sons Company (founded in 1849)—and credited with the invention of the thread spool—merged in 1926 with the Belding Brothers Company (established 1857); Corticelli joined in 1932. Belding Heminway still produces fine threads under the Belding Corticelli name, and a kitten lives on as the company's corporate symbol even today.

Unusual cat-shaped calendars were given free to customers for many years. They kept the Corticelli name at the fingertips of women who used the company's products. Calendars shown are from 1905 and 1907. The cat figure on the right is a counter-top card; the story of how silk is made is printed on the back.

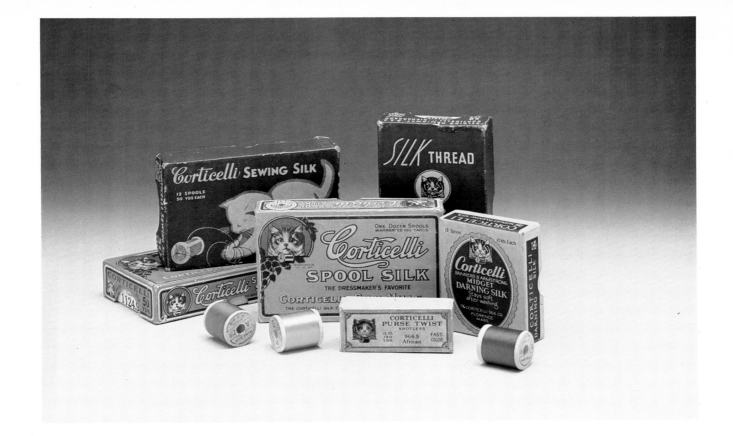

A selection of Corticelli boxes (*above*) illustrates the use of the Corticelli kitten in packaging. Thread spools used around 1920 also displayed tiny kitten faces stamped into the wood on one end. *Below:* Eye-catching signs helped promote Corticelli thread in stores and fabric shops across America. This one, dated 1903 and made of cardboard, measures 21″ x 11″.

Mr. Smith said, "Feed the kitty," in his sleep, and so, say the lyrics of this 1908 song, his wife thought he kept a kitten at his office. But the words really tell of an all-too-familiar concern— how to make ends meet when faced with many hands outstretched for money. Comedy songs like this were particularly popular during the 1900–20 era of show business. Lew Dockstader's photo on the sheet music cover indicates that "Feed the Kitty" was performed in the well-known promoter's traveling minstrel shows.

Someone who exclaimed, "That's the cat's pajamas!" in the 1920s really meant, "That's terrific!" The slang phrase was so popular, it is not surprising that music with that title soon followed. The pajama-clad cats on the cover of this 1922 sheet music brought the title to life, and the melody of this novelty selection brought many pianos alive as well. Piano solos were popular in the early 1920s both for parlor entertainment and in vaudeville.

"Dere aint gon'er be no leavin's"

This advertising postcard was given to visitors at the 1907 Jamestown Exposition. It advertised Egg-O-See fruit-flavored wheat flakes, which were introduced in 1903 by the Battle Creek Breakfast Food Company of Quincy, Illinois. Egg-O-See advertising said that it kept the blood cool and, if substituted for meat during hot summer weather, would improve the consumer's disposition! The illustration of the hungry dog and cats also appeared in Egg-O-See magazine advertising and on store signs from 1905 to 1907. The company and its cereals did not survive; despite its unusual claims and its advertised "germproof packaging," Egg-O-See was no longer sold by 1930.

Many companies produced white lead paint in the late 1800s. The Carter White Lead Company created the colorful advertisement at right for its brand and had a prominent lithography company print it on metal signs. The paint was called "white lead" because one of its main ingredients was the white powder formed when lead corrodes. The "Old Dutch" process mentioned on the sign refers to a competitive product—another white paint first produced in Holland. In 1906, the Carter White Lead Company was purchased by The National Lead Company, now known as NL Industries.

A CATCHY CATASTROPHE.

ROLLING ALONG.

BEECHAM'S PILLS are pleasantly coated, and being round, they will roll. They have already rolled into every English-speaking country in the world, and they are still rolling. All sufferers from indigestion, flatulency, constipation, sick headache, and all other forms of stomach and liver troubles have now this famous and inexpensive remedy within their reach. They enjoy the largest sale of any proprietary medicine in the world. Price, 25 cents; of all druggists. New York Depot, 365 Canal Street.

☞ Complying with general request, Beecham's Pills will in future for the United States be covered with a

P. 1

Quickly Soluble, Pleasant Coating,

completely disguising the taste of the Pill without in any way impairing its efficacy.

When wooden crates of Tom Cat California oranges or lemons were shipped across the country, an imposing feline stood guard on the labels. The Tom Cat brand first appeared in 1922, and the delightfully colorful cat design could be seen well into the modern era of cardboard packing boxes. The now-defunct Orosi Foothills Citrus Association belonged to the California Fruit Growers Exchange—a growers' cooperative that first used the Sunkist trademark in 1908. So the Sunkist symbol appeared along with Tom Cat on the label shown above (ca. 1930), as it did on other members' labels over the years. The Tom Cat brand represented Orosi's top grade; lesser-quality fruit was sold under the Fido name—which pictured a dog on the label! More than eight thousand U.S. citrus growers now use the famous trademark of Sunkist Growers, Inc.

Playful cats drew attention to Beecham's Pills, a laxative, in this 1891 advertisement. The pills were developed in the 1850s by Thomas Beecham, an English entrepreneur, who had advertised this popular Victorian medicine more than fourteen thousand times before 1900.
Beecham's Pills were introduced in the United States in 1888; in keeping with the company's progressive sales philosophy, a sugar coating was added to satisfy American tastes. Today, Thomas Beecham's business has evolved into Beecham Group p.l.c., a diversified British company with more than two hundred products sold worldwide—including pharmaceuticals, cosmetics, and household products.

Cats caught in the act of being cats helped the National Carbon Company, Inc., promote Eveready flashlight batteries on these beautifully illustrated advertising posters. A series of about a dozen posters was produced from the mid-1930s to the late 1940s, and some of the illustrations also appeared in the company's magazine advertising. The sheet music for the popular 1921 melody "Kitten on the Keys" is propped on the piano in the poster on the left (also see page 80). Eveready batteries are now produced by the Union Carbide Corporation.

Behind the cartoon cats on this 1915 sheet music cover is a delightful comedy song. The lyrics tell of noisy nocturnal cats (a favorite comic theme) and how their moonlight serenades disturbed a family for years—until Nellie sang the opera *Il Trovatore* and all the cats disappeared. The photo vignette at the lower left represents an early promotional tactic—music publishers often reproduced likenesses of popular entertainers on song sheet covers, whether or not the performers had any connection with the song, in the hope of influencing people to buy a copy of the sheet music.

ACKNOWLEDGMENTS

We would like to thank the people who helped us in the creation of this book:

Jane Jordan Browne, who had enough faith in *The Cat Made Me Buy It!* to represent us; Brandt Aymar, editor at Crown Publishers, Inc., whose enthusiasm made the book a reality; the staffs of the U.S. Copyright Office, Library of Congress, and the Department of Commerce, Office of Patents and Trademarks, for generously assisting us through their maze of files; the people at the many city and state governmental offices we contacted, as well as the staffs of dozens of museums, libraries, chambers of commerce, historical societies, and trade associations, various town historians; Ken Kapson for his knowledge and energy, without whose assistance the writing of this book would have been much more difficult; Russell Yanow, for constant encouragement; and the many antiques dealers from whom we have purchased examples of cats in advertising over the years, for without them our collections would not have been possible.

We also appreciate the courtesy and cooperation of the following companies, which granted permission to reproduce their advertising, with special thanks for the efforts of numerous corporate executives and archivists who made historical information available to us—especially Bruce Klein of the Belding Heminway Company, Inc., and Shirley Jackson of Jockey International, Inc.

(4) The Nestle-LeMur Company. (11) Sam Fox Publishing Company, Inc. and Sebco, Inc. (17) Courtesy of the Archives, The Coca-Cola Company. (18) The Valspar Corporation, successor to the business of John W. Masury & Son, has granted permission to print this advertisement. (19) J. Strickland & Company. (20–21) J. L. Prescott Co. (22) By permission of J. W. Spear & Sons p.l.c. (23) Parker Brothers games reprinted by permission. (24) Coats & Clark, Inc. (27) Wm. Wrigley Jr. Company. (28 top) Used by permission of Westwood Pharmaceuticals. (28 bottom) Dray Enterprises, Inc. (30–35) Courtesy

Jockey International, Inc. (37) Warner-Lambert Company. (38–39) Cat's Paw name and logos are trademarks of The Biltright Corporation, Chelsea, Massachusetts. (42–43) Copyright © 1984 Kellogg Company, all rights reserved. Used with permission. (45) Copyright 1913, (renewed) Warner Bros., Inc. All rights reserved. Used by permission. (46) Lorillard, a Division of Loew's Theatres, Inc. (47) The Procter & Gamble Company. (48–49) Dr. A. C. Daniels, Inc. (51 left) By permission of Uniroyal, Inc. (51 right) Ethyl Corporation. (56–67) With permission of the Chessie System Railroads. (58) American Thread Company. (59) Sterling Drug Inc. (60 bottom) Sanford Corporation. (60 top, 61) Dennison Manufacturing Company. (62) Cooper Laboratories, Inc. (63) Parker Brothers games reprinted by permission. (64) Faultless Starch/Bon Ami Company. (65) Olivilo® is a registered trademark of Purex Corporation. (66) The B. F. Goodrich Company. (67) International Silver Company. (71) The New Home Sewing Machine Company. (73) Courtesy of The Procter & Gamble Company. (78 top) Milton Bradley Company. (78 bottom) Parker Brothers games reprinted by permission. (79) The Flintkote Company. (80 bottom) Copyright 1921 by Mills Music, Inc. Copyright renewed. Used with permission. All rights reserved. (80 top) LePage's Incorporated. (82–87) Belding Heminway Company, Inc. (88) Copyright Larry Spier, Inc., New York, N.Y. Reprinted by permission. (91) NL Chemicals, Div. of NL Industries. (92) Beecham Group p.l.c. (93) SUNKIST is a registered trademark of Sunkist Growers, Inc., Sherman Oaks, Calif. 91423. (94–95) Courtesy of the Battery Products Division, Union Carbide Corp. (96) Shapiro, Bernstein & Co., Inc. Used by permission.

Every effort has been made to contact the copyright and trademark owners or their representatives. If there have been any omissions, please notify us and we will rectify them in future printings.